CALLED TO MINISTRY

Best Practices for Women Clergy

by

Brenda Billingy

Title: *Called to Ministry: Best Practices for Women Clergy*

Author: Brenda Billingy
Publisher: Pacific Press Publishing
Place of Publication: Nampa, ID
Year of Publication: 2015

ISBN-10: 0-692-45981-2
ISBN-13: 978-0-692-45981-2

Medium: Print, Paperback
Published in the United States

INTRODUCTION

Pastor Brenda Billingy
Associate Ministerial Director
North American Division of Seventh-day Adventists

The last admonition given us in the book of James is very powerful. The apostle writes, "Remember this: Whoever turns a sinner from the error of their way will save them from death and cover over a multitude of sins" (James 5:20, NIV). Conversion is helpful, but I believe there is another process that is often overlooked—prevention. "Prevention is better than cure." To be able to prevent someone from error would certainly avoid a multitude of unintended sins.

Thinking creatively about this concept and transferring it into the pastoral context allowed me to initiate the Holy Spirit's suggestion for helping female clergy avoid costly mistakes by learning from the best practices offered by other female colleagues in ministry. Each pastor has been asked to share one "best practice" that lends itself to a successful ministry, something that, if incorporated, would help to prevent errors that could potentially deter or distract a pastor. After all, we will never live long enough to make all the possible mistakes in ministry, so why not learn from others and jump over the hoops the enemy has designed to destroy ministry?

On behalf of all the authors, we humbly submit these best practices, realizing that the ministry journey of a female pastor is quite unique. We pray that the suggestions given will prevent pastors from unnecessary errors, help to save a soul, and hide a multitude of faults and sins. I appreciate every pastor who has shared candidly, and I pray that we leave a strong legacy of spiritual practices and procedures that will have a positive influence for generations to come.

Continue to be blessed, so that you can be a blessing.

LISTENING FEMALE PASTORS

As pastors, we are blessed with dynamic resources—sitting in our pews! Many times we struggle with how to get things done when God has already provided a church member who can be the human resource to complete the task. Sometimes, we hesitate to ask because we don't want to seem vulnerable or incapable. But "no woman lives on an island by herself;" no one can do everything that needs to be done. We need each other to survive!

I can recall many times when I was "stuck" on how to proceed in a given situation. I may have had the idea or the vision, but I needed some help in implementation. I have discovered that sharing the idea with my members allows them to dream with me, and before long, if I listen carefully, they will often share with me brilliant solutions as well as the personnel to accomplish the task. If we stay in a mode of discernment, the Holy Spirit will tell us whom we should share our ideas with, and when we are talking to that person, He will tune our ears to listen attentively for the divine solutions.

I shared this book project with a woman in my congregation. I wanted to write about the art of listening. Even as we were discussing the concept on the phone, she was already pouring forth ideas about how listening relates to female pastors. In essence, because of her giftedness in teaching listening skills, she was able to be the resource person I needed to help write this article. I had to be willing to listen and be obedient to the voice of God through Marva, as He shared His ideas for "Listening Female Pastors." I'm grateful for the human resources that the Lord places in our pews. Please enjoy and listen (take heed) to her comments below.

Be Quick to Listen

Marva Shand-McIntosh

TEXT: "Wherefore my beloved brethren, let every man [woman] be swift to listen, slow to speak, slow to wrath" (James 1:19).

You are called to be a prophetic voice to the people God places in your life. Mark Batterson said, "The key to discovering (and using) your prophetic voice is to cultivate a prophetic ear." This means learning to listen. In a succinct definition, John Maxwell said, "Hearing is a function of the ear, but listening is a function of the will." Listening is not easy because it requires time, discipline, right attitude, training, and humility.

As a spiritual leader, effective female pastors must cultivate the ability to listen to God, to others, and to one's self.

LISTENING TO GOD. In our communication with God we need to make room for Him to speak. Prayer is *talking* to God, however Bible reading and meditation are powerful ways of *listening* to God. Listening is a spiritual discipline that leads to obedience. "Obedience is God's love language" because He said, "If you love me keep my commandments" (John 14:15). It is so comforting to know that our Almighty God knows that we are sinners yet He listens to us as if we are saints.

LISTENING TO OTHERS is a gift of service, and it is also a time of learning. In addition, at times female pastors will get the opportunity to listen for others. That is, God will speak to you regarding the affairs of someone else just because you are willing to listen. As a leader, keep in mind that listening sends a message of respect, and it is also a powerful motivational strategy.

LISTENING TO YOURSELF. Women have a special portion of the gift of intuition. Unfortunately, too many times we override our intuition and then say, "I should have . . . " At times our intuitions serve as a unique veil of protection for us females. Use it.

In your daily life, speak blessing so that when it comes back to your ear you will be blessed by your own words in return. The opposite is also true. Lying, slander, gossip, and other mean words also come back to the ear of the speaker—as a curse.

Finally, challenge yourself to listen first, be the first one to listen, and listen quickly. ***Be quick to listen: that's what godly female ministers do.***

Brenda Billingy, Senior Pastor
Metropolitan Seventh-day Adventist Church, Hyattsville, Maryland
Associate Ministerial Director, North American Division of Seventh-day Adventists

Marva Shand-McIntosh
Designer of Adventurer Listening honor
Founder, "I Love to Listen Day—May 16"

ADD ME TO YOUR FRIENDS LIST

Elizabeth Pule
Associate Pastor, Ottawa Seventh-day Adventist Church
Ottawa, Ontario, Canada

In these days of social media and its influence, it is always funny to hear people talk about having over 10,000 "friends" or "followers" on Facebook or Twitter. I mean, you aren't *really* getting together for dinner or tea with 90 percent of those people—so why even bother? I think the reason many people today request friendship on social media is because they want fellowship. They want people to "like" their status updates and ever-changing profile pictures. They seek acknowledgment of their daily decisions or comfort in their mistakes.

In all of us, there is a desire to make connections. I have worked as a church pastor and a school chaplain, and most of my time has been spent making connections with people—starting friendships with individuals, growing those friendships to where I can share Jesus with them, helping them identify their own gifts for ministry, and then giving them opportunities to use their gifts for the Lord. I find that when people are actively engaged in ministry and service, their relationship with Jesus comes alive.

As a pastor and a chaplain, I have always made an effort to establish relationships with young people. We've spent time talking over biblical themes, practical applications of those themes, practicing preaching, reading the Bible, and praying. Those times of studying God's Word and making it relevant to them made a noticeable difference in their lives and in the lives of their peers.

To hear God's promises is always a blessing; to listen to a young person preach the gospel is absolutely amazing! At our church we hold regular youth preaching partnerships and have the young people share their sermons during divine service and other programs. Last year, the youth planned and presented two evangelistic series in which they shared their testimonies of how God has changed their lives. We even held some of the meetings on a secular university campus so students could invite their friends and co-workers and explain to them how life is better with Jesus.

Sure, there are challenges, as there always will be in ministry. But God is so good! We have seen people give their lives to the Lord in baptism, because they have witnessed how He can use all kinds of people to do His work—men, women, old and young. So please, go ahead and make connections on Instagram, Pinterest, and Tumblr, because you never know how the Holy Spirit can grow those friendships.

The Bible says, "To the elders among you, I appeal as a fellow elder and a witness of Christ's sufferings who also will share in the glory to be revealed: Be shepherds of God's flock that is under your care, watching over them—not because you must, but because you are willing, as God wants you to be; not pursuing dishonest gain, but eager to serve; not lording it over those entrusted to you, but being examples to the flock. And when the Chief Shepherd appears, you will receive the crown of glory that will never fade away. In the same way, you who are younger, submit yourselves to your elders. All of you, clothe yourselves with humility toward one another, because, 'God opposes the proud but shows favor to the humble' " (1 Peter 5:1-5, NIV).

Our heavenly Father has entrusted us with a blessed responsibility to nurture and disciple those in our care. Let us mentor our young people to preach the good news. Let us do so with a glad heart and ask the Holy Spirit for renewed strength. Our young people are willing and able to craft a sermon, write a powerful testimony, and reach people we would never have the opportunity of connecting with. So the next time you prepare a sermon or make evangelism plans, make an intentional effort to connect with a young person and mentor him or her along the way.

Blessings and hugs!

BABY DEDICATIONS EQUAL GREAT EVANGELISTIC OPPORTUNITIES

Donna Holland
Senior Pastor, White Memorial Seventh-day Adventist Church
Portland, Maine

Have you ever wished several new families would attend your church on Sabbath—families who have never attended before? There is a way to potentially begin lasting relationships with families who are not yet church members—by having a service to dedicate their infants or older children. Dedicating a child isn't dependent on church membership, so you may freely hold a dedication service even if the parents are not members.

Anyone who wants to raise their child to love and serve Jesus needs to be encouraged to do that, whether or not they continue to attend my church. However, I consider any parent who approaches me and requests a baby dedication service to be a good interest. I have baptized parents who asked for a baby dedication, and I have later baptized children who were dedicated at the request of parents who were not baptized members.

Besides parents, baby dedications bring into the church friends and extended family members who might never enter the church otherwise. Treat them royally! Have the parents bring the baby (or child) up front, then invite all the extended family and friends to gather around them to indicate they are supporting the parents in this endeavor.

At the close of the dedication, present the parents with a certificate of dedication and a gift that will help them remember this service or help the child's spiritual growth. I like to use a basket and put in it things such as spiritual baby books, religious "quiet toys" that the child can use during church, as well as a small New Testament in which I have filled out the "Presented To . . ." page. I tell the family that the baby will not remember this day, but this Bible is something they can keep to let the child know he or she was dedicated to the Lord on this day. If the child is older, use a religious storybook or a religious coloring books and crayons or colored pencils. You may even include a small stuffed animal. The gift basket is generally unexpected (unless the parents have seen you perform other baby dedications) and will be a pleasant surprise. This helps bond the family to the church and also gives the parents something to help the child spiritually.

If you have a church school in connection with your church, you can give the family a baby T-shirt imprinted with "Future Student of [name of school]." This is great advertising for the school—both to the family and to everyone in church that day.

Take pictures of the baby dedication—lots of pictures! Make sure you get a picture of the whole group of extended family and friends who came for the dedication. After the service, send these pictures to the parents. If possible, give them a CD or other electronic media with the pictures on it. This will allow them to share the pictures with as many family members as they wish, and from an evangelistic point of view, the more people involved the better. If you have a bulletin board, post the pictures on it (with the individuals' permission, of course). Seeing their pictures when they (hopefully) return to church will be a positive for most people. It will help them to feel like this is their church.

If you do this and make the dedication service special, chances are good that the parents will tell their friends about having their baby dedicated, and that their friends may also want to have a dedication service for their children. Rarely have I had a dedication service for someone who never came back to church. However, I have baptized family members of the child/baby I dedicated.

Females are generally considered more adept at forming caring relationships, so why not use that in ministry? Give your ministry that extra personal touch whenever you can!

CHANGING ATTITUDES

Shirley Allen
Associate Pastor
Sunnyside Seventh-day Adventist Church

The church where I serve has a history of female pastors. I am at least the fourth. Despite this, I found, however, that many of the church members didn't view a female pastor as a "pastor." The reason? Like me, the previous lady pastors had pastored with their husbands.

I realized the privilege I had to serve with my husband. There are a number of female pastors who would love to pastor as associates with their husbands, but the opportunities to do so are few and far between. My predecessors had set the bar high as female pastors of vision and purpose.

It was not until my husband was asked to serve as a conference administrator, and I remained at our church as a pastor, that the members' attitude toward female pastors changed—little by little. Several of the members thought I would leave the church when my husband did. Gradually, they began to realize that I had a calling, too, and that I would stay until the Lord led me elsewhere.

Being a woman pastor in this church after my husband left has had its challenges. I have needed to be respectful of new ideas, thoughts, and vision. I've developed as part of a team composed of the senior and associate pastors. Now, after five years of pastoring together, we realize how we complement one another's strengths and weaknesses.

One of the joys I have had is building teams with multiple layers as we continually recruit volunteers for the ministries for which I am responsible. These teams are a tremendous support group for me and our ministries. Their prayers and their ministry give our work depth and hold me accountable.

Another joy for me in ministry is discovering how someone has been gifted and then finding opportunities for the person to serve in that area. I often get to visit with new members. It thrills my heart to see them getting involved in a ministry and sharing their hearts and talents with the church and the community.

I think female pastors notice details and care in ways that can be supportive of members in a ministry that transcends gender and age.

CHILDREN'S MINISTRY

Shawna Campbell
Children's Pastor
Loma Linda University Church

Energy! Laughter! Playfulness! Learning! Children have a way of keeping our spirits young and re-energizing our passion for Jesus. Maybe it's their innocence or their enthusiasm, but the youthfulness of children rejuvenates me and makes me feel young at heart! What a blessing and honor it is reaching children through ministry for God!

As Children's Ministry Pastor, my desire is to make Jesus real and relevant to all the children in our church as well as to those in our community. One of the most realistic ways to draw children into a relationship with Jesus is through a well-planned, creative Vacation Bible School. Today, many children in our communities are not growing up in homes that place Jesus first. Our society is so materialistic that most children know nothing of God or the Bible. Many of them will come to Vacation Bible School, and that is our opportunity to reach out to them with new concepts that will help them develop a faith in God. It's an awesome responsibility for us to take maximum advantage of this teachable moment of learning.

And so, my challenge, as Children's Ministry Pastor, was: How do I use the few hours of Vacation Bible School to impress these children with the gospel? The answer was simple: Make every moment both interesting and intentional, filled with knowledge and activities that the Holy Spirit could use to impress these young minds.

Our staff evaluated the pre-planned VBS program and made some changes. We eliminated the Snack Rotation to maximize our time. Instead of giving a full rotation for preparing snacks, we gave out bags of crackers and fruit during the Bible Story Rotation when the children were quietly seated. In its place, we added a Prayer Rotation. The children made prayer boxes and filled them with their prayer requests. They started prayer journals to record their gratitude and repentance and to begin a dialogue with God. They also spent time praying for others, both locally and worldwide.

We also adjusted our Craft Rotation so that it would have a focus on outreach. Instead of making a craft for themselves, the children made things for others. For example, they followed a recipe to measure beans, lentils, and rice—along with spices and herbs—to make soup bags for our church ministry, "Meals on Wheels." On another day, the children decorated labels and bookmarks to include in books that the church was distributing in the neighborhood and in various shelters. They also decorated flip-flops and brought shoes for a local elementary school located in a poor area of town. The children made cards for patients at the Veterans Hospital and drew pictures for shut-ins and seniors. They were being taught to reach out to other kids and people in need; the focus was on others.

We have a responsibility to our youth and children to show them a glimpse of Jesus and teach them how to empathize with others in our community through service. Together, we can train children to be the hands and feet of Jesus. When Vacation Bible School was finally over, we warmly invited all the children to continue the fun of service and the good work they had done by coming each Saturday morning to a weekly "VBS." Only eternity will reveal the results of this outreach!

COURAGE

Dúane Schoonard, MS
Associate Pastor
Lakeview Seventh-day Adventist Church
Counselor/Chaplain, Georgia-Cumberland Conference

Courage is multi-faceted.

Physical courage demands that I confront existential fears. When my daughter chose to jump out of a plane, it demanded physical courage of the highest order. It also took emotional courage for me to let her do it—and even more courage to watch her do it!

Emotional courage is the ability to be authentic and real while feeling vulnerable—to show up when it might hurt to do so; to love in the midst of rejection; to be present in the midst of pain; to feel the depth of loss when you are broken; to forgive while being mistreated.

When religious or societal norms support injustice or abuse, social courage stands for principle, righteousness, justice, and mercy. Dorothea Dix, of the early 1800s, refused to be quiet when she saw first-hand people with mental illnesses being treated inhumanely. At that time, the mentally ill were housed in jails with criminals. When asked to teach a Sunday School lesson in the local prison in the dead of winter, Dix discovered that there was no heat, inadequate clothing, and no blankets. She confronted the jailer, who stated, "They don't feel the cold."

Speaking with authority, she said, "If I'm cold, they are cold. Get them some blankets!"

Until her death, Dorothea Dix advocated for compassionate treatment of the mentally ill. Before the Massachusetts Supreme Court she argued, "I proceed, gentlemen, briefly to call your attention to the present state of insane persons confined within this Commonwealth, in cages, stalls, pens! Chained, naked, beaten with rods, and lashed into obedience." That is social courage.

To have spiritual or moral courage is to live counter-culturally—to live with absolute integrity, without manipulation or political posturing. It is not only to demand that of myself, but to call people to live in accordance with biblical principles.

It is this moral courage that is most lacking in Christian leadership today. We are content to pamper the saints and bury the dead, rather than demand of ourselves true righteousness. The least common denominator—those most unwilling to change, those with the narrowest of views—are given power in our lives and in our churches, because we have not the moral courage to stand against the tide of spiritual apathy and tradition. As a result, the church fails to fulfill its mission of healing the brokenhearted, of lightening the burdens of those who are oppressed, and of removing the chains that entrap people who long to be free.

If we are to survive as a church we must have ideas, vision, and courage. These qualities are not generally forged by committees, but by confronting our own mind and consciousness and by following the convictions of the

Holy Spirit. Rolla May says, "The opposite of courage in our society is not cowardice, it is conformity." Moral courage demands that we stand between the voice of the crowd and our own convictions and do what is right because it is right. Moral courage costs dearly; that is why it is called courage. But without this type of courage we perpetuate dysfunctional churches and support spiritual apathy. As ministers, we are commissioned to call those entrusted to our care to higher levels of spiritual, emotional, and relational health. We are called to place priority on nurturing healthy communities where the transforming power of the gospel is seen and celebrated. We are called to be agents of change, not for the sake of change or being different, but to reach out with hope and help to a world thrashing about in fear and anxiety. As long as we continue to maintain the status quo, we will continue to become less and less relevant and, therefore, have no need to exist.

This classic statement of Ellen White still rings true: "The greatest want of the world is the want of [wo]men--[wo]men who will not be bought or sold; [wo]men who in their inmost souls are true and honest; [wo]men who do not fear to call sin by its right name; [wo]men whose conscience is as true to duty as the needle to the pole; [wo]men who will stand for the right though the heavens fall."—*Education*, p. 57.

GROWING A COMMUNITY

Wendy Witas
Family Life Pastor
Pacific Union College Seventh-day Adventist Church

While teaching kindergarten years ago, I had a very active little girl named, Alyssa. She had black bobbed hair, sparkling Asian eyes, and a sense of mischief that was a constant challenge. I was trying to help my students learn to be a loving community. So as we talked and shared at "circle time," I would say, "See, when we share the swing, we are being 'community.' When we share a toy, we are being 'community.' " For my active Alyssa this concept was especially difficult.

That was to change on one glorious day. During "center time" Alyssa yelled out with gusto, "Teacher, I am being community." She was proudly grinning at a boy in the class whom she had let sit at the computer and take a turn. We all celebrated, because a five-year-old girl was recognizing the beautiful picture of sharing, thinking of others, and meeting their needs. We were "community."

Some of our churches are sadly lacking community. According to Stephen Ilardi, Ph.D., "Remarkably, 25 percent of Americans have no meaningful social support at all—not a single person they can confide in. And over half of all Americans report having no close confidants or friends outside their immediate family. The situation is much worse today than it was when similar data were gathered in 1985. (At that time, only 10 percent of Americans were completely alone.)"—*The Depression Cure.*

Unfortunately, our churches sometimes reflect this challenge. I have not been a pastor long; my training has been as an educator. However, I have seen the sad reality that isolation and lack of community is prevalent with our children, families, and older church members.

Reflecting on these challenges in my own congregation, I saw a fragmented group made up of an older retired community, college students, faculty and staff of the college, and their children—as well as a few community people. The isolation was visible in the distance people sat from each other in church. Support for families was lacking. Community was almost dead with the exception of a few pocket groups. One woman told me that we may be an Adventist congregation, but we are a broken, isolated group that rarely socializes together.

When my husband and I arrived at our current church, there were few children. Most services were either very formal (first service) or informal (second service)—nothing in between. Hebrews 10:24, 25 came to mind: "And let us consider how to stir up one another to love and good works, not neglecting to meet together, as is the habit of some, but encouraging one another, and all the more as you see the Day drawing near."—RSV, emphasis supplied.

To combat this isolation and lack of support, my team and I prayed for methods that would welcome children and their families and provide ways to meet together, play together, work together, and worship together. Our number one goal was to plan engaging, family-friendly, multi-generational events that would make our church family more community friendly and supportive—like Jesus wants us to be.

Our first step was to have a simple Children's Church. A handful of folks attended with their children. With my education background, I knew that to truly engage children and families, the Children's Church needed to be hands-on and as active as possible, so kids would learn by doing.

We chose themes for our Children's Church that had stations for kids to experience the Bible story being presented. This would include things like riding a boat with Jonah and feeling the wind and water splashing in their faces while hearing the sounds of thunder and storm. The children could go inside the belly of a whale (aka: a tent made to look like a whale) which had smelly, fishy things inside it. In another corner we had the college Biology department share artifacts from the ocean in a museum-like setting. For preschoolers, there were tide pools where they could find fish and shells while playing in sand and water. Everything needed to work at creating an environment in which children and parents heard, touched, smelled, and experienced the wonders of God and the biblical story—in this case the story of Jonah. This was the final Children's Church in May of my first year at this church. We had over 300 people come, including community visitors with their children. I have been so thrilled seeing our family attendance grow as we have worked hard to create a family-friendly environment and community. Church attendance has grown as well, because we are becoming a community.

God is moving in powerful ways as we think outside the box with creative ways to engage our families and kids. One of our recent events was a "Wild West Harvest Fest," which gave the community a safe alternative to Halloween. Over 800 people, including church members and non-church members, attended. It was a huge success with young and old playing together in a God-friendly community. Later we had a community "Light in the Night" event, lighting the church courtyard and having a simple, live nativity scene. We also have a family vespers one Friday evening a month. These events, in addition to worshiping together on Sabbaths, have helped to bridge the isolation gap. Our community is growing with folks encouraging each other and becoming a true church family that works, plays, and worships together. I want to yell out, like my little girl, Alyssa, "We are being community!" Praise God!

I pray that God will bring continued success in ministry by helping our church learn to be a community that loves each other, reaching across all generations to find common ground. Jesus said, "By this all men will know that you are my disciples, if you have love for one another."—John 13:35, RSV.

And love does not exist without community.

I REMEMBER OPAL

Raewyn Jean Hankins
Senior Pastor, Victorville SDA Church of Green Tree

Opal Erfurth. I can't forget her name now, because somewhere along the way, we *did* forget about her. I say "we," not because remembering was my responsibility or that of the pastors who came before me, but because she belonged to us, and "we," collectively, forgot. Perhaps she just drifted away, as did 28 percent of former members surveyed in a recent study presented at the NAD 2014 Year-end Meetings. Maybe Opal felt she couldn't live up to our standards (as did 24 percent) or was angry with us (like 19 percent). Perhaps we had simply become irrelevant to Opal's life (as we were for 17 percent). Possibly no one contacted her when she stopped coming to church (as was true for 40 percent).

Whatever the reason Opal was missing, when I knocked on her door, the woman who answered was surprised to see me.

As a pastor, I figured it would take till Jesus comes for me to visit everyone in our church (about 600 members and friends), so one "Connect Sabbath," we divided up the church list into zones (based on the last four extra digits of the zip code) and sent out everyone who would go. (I got the idea from my uncle who pastored in South Africa). Previously, we had mailed a letter letting the people know we were coming. We had prepared a gift to give them—a mug containing items saying, "You're part of the body." When we went out the second time, nine months later, we took a package of Corn Nuts with a note attached saying, "We're stopping by to say 'God is nuts about you. It may sound corny but it's absolutely true!' ").

That afternoon, we heard comments such as, "I've been a member for thirty-five years and have never had a visit." "It's been fifteen years since I've been to your church, but I'd come if someone gave me a ride." "I've been gone for four weeks, and no one noticed." "I'd like Bible studies." "I was watching 3ABN and felt like coming back to church today—and then you showed up!"

Opal was on my list. When I asked for her, the woman at the door said, "She died."

Caught off guard, I replied, "I'm so sorry to hear that!"

Her daughter-in-law looked at me and responded flatly, "She died six years ago."

It was too late to take back my words and too late to connect with Opal. Perhaps, if we had shown we cared sooner, Opal would have been "likely" (as were 36 percent of those surveyed) or "somewhat likely" (21 percent) to reconnect. Instead, Opal had disappeared, then died, and we hadn't found out for years.

Today, our church has elders caring for each geographical "Connect Zone" and a newly-baptized member who mails birthday cards to members (using information from our database). I call members and friends on their birthdays and anniversaries, asking how they're celebrating and how I can be praying for them during this next year of their life. Those calls and connections have led to people reinvesting in a relationship with us.

It's still possible for someone to stop coming to church and slip away unnoticed. We haven't figured out a way to close the back door. But every day, Opal's name reminds me that people are our most precious resource and our greatest treasure. Opal is one of those buried treasures for whom the Son of Man sold everything (see Matthew 13:44). I can't forget her name—or the priority of looking for the ones Christ loves.

LADIES FIRST

Rebecca Davis
Associate Pastor, Berean Seventh-day Adventist Church

We walked into the gym that day with our hair tied down under scarves, wearing baggy clothes and an intense expression on our faces. It was our first time to play basketball at this particular gym. We were greeted by a group of older, beautiful women—the ones we would be playing against. These ladies were members of one of the first women's basketball teams for the University of Louisville. They immediately called our attention to the way we looked and dressed. And they proceeded to teach us a lesson I have never forgotten. These beautiful, older, ball-playing women told us we were not allowed to play basketball in their gym looking like we did. One woman turned to us and said, "Remember, you are ladies before anything." From that day, I never approached the game of basketball the same.

In a male-dominated field like ministry, the temptation is to look like "them"—preach like them, dress like them, walk like them, do ministry like them, and sound like them. We women pastors often shy away from being ladylike, because ultimately we want to be accepted by them. Subconsciously, our rationale becomes, "The more we act like them, the less we'll stand out, which in turn will lead to finding a place among them."

As a woman in ministry, you don't have to wear a bland suit. It's okay to wear nice dresses. It's okay to be in style. (There is one rule to this, however: Always choose clothes that flatter you over clothes that are in style. Just because it's in style doesn't mean it's the style for you.)

When you speak, you don't have to lower your voice so much that you don't even recognize yourself. You don't have to sit in the corner; you can sit at the decision-making table. You don't have to be obsolete or marginalized; you can (and will) be at the forefront with class, elegance, and finesse. Your acceptance is found in God who called you as a woman! He did not make a mistake in this! When men, as fully men, and women, as fully women, come together, we will finish this work—together!

I want to challenge every one of you women in ministry to embrace your femininity. This will be one of your "best practices" for ministry. I want to challenge you to embrace gentleness, embrace beauty, embrace style, embrace supporting other women, embrace confidence, embrace security, and embrace all that makes you "woman!" Don't walk on the court, if you will, with a scarf on! Walk on confidently and plant your feet firmly in your three-and-a-half-inch heels (or flats) and preach, teach, counsel, and plan ministries around issues that speak to your emphatic heart!

Remember, you are a lady before anything.

LISTEN AS YOU PREACH

Ida Smith
Associate Pastor, Downsview Seventh-day Adventist Church
Toronto, Canada

I believe that our practice, as preachers, must be to pray and listen as we prepare our sermons to present to our congregations each week or month, as the case may be. I have learned over my four years of pastoral ministry not only to listen to the voice of God as I prepare my sermons, but to listen to His voice and obey Him in the midst of my preaching.

This has never been an easy thing for me to do, since my natural inclination is to stick to my sermon notes. However, I have discovered that each time I deviate from my sermon notes to carry out the instructions I believe God is giving me through the Holy Spirit, the response is always positive. It's easy to ignore or to disobey God's voice speaking to me while I'm preaching, because He often instructs me to carry out duties which seem illogical and unusual. But interestingly enough, although the instructions often appear this way, there is always at least one individual in the congregation who brings me some confirmation to let me know that it was God's voice speaking, as opposed to my own inclination.

For example, one Sabbath I was conducting a communion service, and at the close of the service I felt an overwhelming impression to make an appeal. "Make an appeal for someone to re-dedicate himself or herself to Me," the inner voice said. "This could be their last communion service."

I must admit that it was a great struggle for me to carry out this instruction. Self was in the way. What will people think about me? I thought. This has never happened here before. People will think I'm going out of my mind; they are going to report this to the lead pastor. What will he think of me?

All these thoughts and more flashed through my mind. Finally the words came to mind, Obey God rather than men. And through the power of the Spirit I made the conscious decision to carry out the instruction given.

I cannot recall everything I said, but from the look on the faces of the people in the congregation I could see that they were uncomfortable. An altar call at the end of the communion service is unheard of in this congregation; maybe you have never heard of it, either. But who are we to say what God will instruct us to do or when He will instruct us to do it or how He will say it should be done? I believe that our role is to listen and obey.

Well, at the end of the service, one lady, a member of the congregation and a faithful member of our vibrant prayer group, met me at the door and told me she was blessed.

In all the years I've been conducting communion services and preaching, I cannot recall that this woman has ever told me that before. By the way, she was the only one who confessed that to me that day. The Lord knew I needed some kind of confirmation.

One month later this dear sister became ill and was hospitalized. I visited her and prayed with her—and then left on vacation. Sad to say, while I was on vacation, she passed away.

Although I was sad to hear of her passing, I thanked God that He used me to bless her on her last communion day. I felt happy that I had listened to His instruction to deviate from the norm as I preached that day.

As I reflect on this story, the Bible text that comes to mind is Acts 4:19, "But Peter and John answered and said unto them, Whether it be right in the sight of God to hearken unto you more than unto God, judge ye."—KJV.

My dear pastors, it is certainly better to obey God rather than man.

LOVE LANGUAGE AND GROWING IN THE SPIRIT

Sherry Augustus
Associate Pastor
Ontario Conference of Seventh-day Adventist

"And be not conformed to this world: but be ye transformed by the renewing of your mind, that ye may prove what is that good, and acceptable, and perfect, will of God."—Romans 12:2, KJV.

When I look at me, I see a sanguine/phlegmatic whose love language is *Words of Affirmation and Acts of Service*. The two most important keys to success in ministry are being able to recognize the personality types of those who surround me and identifying the "love language" they "speak." After the presence of the Holy Spirit in my life, these are my two main ways to remain sane (at least in my crazy, sanguine head)!

I find people to be utterly frustrating. People look you in the face and lie. People avoid you when their friends are around. People sabotage your work and reputation. People pretend to agree with you and then conveniently "forget" their conversation with you when they are speaking to someone who disagrees! People feel justified in completely sidestepping privacy to point out your weaknesses in public. People, people, people . . . !

Sometimes knowing *who* I am and *whose* I am isn't enough. Sometimes the severity of the "now" overpowers my humility, and the *me* that nobody sees starts shouting in my head, demanding a stab at the microphone!

What do I do during those times?

I start with prayer, and I end with a quick analysis to determine which combination of personality type and love language is directing the episode I'm currently trapped in! Through this avenue, the Holy Spirit gives me insight into the hidden mindsets and emotions that are driving the discussion, and I am able to address *those* without responding in like manner to the anger and frustration being vomited on me.

This analysis reminds me that a *choleric* likes to have things "my way." A *melancholy* likes things to be "the right way." A *sanguine* likes it "the fun way," and a *phlegmatic* likes it "any way!"[1] The Holy Spirit also gives me much needed peace in the storm by helping me to see that what I am experiencing is a natural part of the areas of weakness that this particular personality type struggles with—and that this is probably one of the things that the Holy Spirit is currently working on! He also reminds me that in my own life, I do not always see the filth in me until it is on its way out.

Analyzing personality types also focuses my attention on the "love language" cues I hear in the complaint. For example, if a person says,

[1] A concise summary of the Personality Types can be found at http://wearegateway.ca/wp-content/uploads/2010/10/PersonalityPlus.pdf. The Personality Plus test is also available on this site.

"You're not listening, and you don't pay attention when I. . . ," I can guess that her love language is *Quality Time*, and I apologize for unintentionally ignoring her. Or when a person says, "You didn't help with. . ." I deduce that her love language is *Acts of Service*, at which point I assure her that I will either make the time to help or find someone else to do so.

My personal love language is *Words of Affirmation*, so my personal feelings may be hurt if someone hurls at me, "What you said was very stupid, because. . ." At this point, however, I can minister to *that person's* need for words of affirmation—and validate her as a valuable member of the team. (Usually she validates me right back, and my hurt feelings are also assuaged.)

Because I can readily admit that I am still under construction, I am more patient with others. My continued prayer is that I will not allow the roaring lion to scare me away from the safety of the Father's protection so that I respond in a way that Satan can use to devour me. I pray that my first reactions will reflect more and more the mind of Christ and less and less the mentality of the world. I continue to pray for spiritual discernment to "prove what is that good, and acceptable, and perfect, will of God."—Romans 12:2.

NURTURE AND ENCOURAGEMENT

Shawn Jackson Moss
Pastor, Bethany Seventh-day Adventist Church
South Central Conference

When asked which single characteristic of my ministry has worked well for me, the honest truth is I had no clue. As I thought more about it, I realized that the truth of the matter is that what works best for me is what we all need—nurture and encouragement. I find that nurture makes connecting relationships easier and allows others to truly relax, be themselves, and know that you ultimately have their best interests in mind.

The best thing about nurture is that no matter how much nurture you give out, you always receive so much more in return.

What is nurture? Nurture can be sharing a meal, chatting about what interests another, or encouraging someone to actually fulfill their dream.

It is caring for and encouraging the growth or development of someone else. It is partnering with another to make something happen in ministry that he or she would not ordinarily have been willing to attempt. It is the absolute desire to see those with whom you work, interact, and fellowship become their truest, best self in service for the Lord.

That is often a tough thing to do if you are someone who has difficulty relinquishing control, because nurture involves giving someone else the reins, allowing someone else to navigate, opening the door for someone else to drive the bus. Nurture requires you to work on your own need to "be in charge," recognizing that Jesus is truly the One in charge and that our job is to follow His lead—even when He is telling us to get out of the way and allow those whom we have the privilege of pastoring to fly free. They can't do it if we are blocking the runway. They can do it if we don't allow them to fly the plane!

Nurture is lovingly training and helping others to develop their God-given gifts and talents to their fullest potential—and then getting out of the way and letting them do what God gave them gifts to do!

That is my best ministry practice, and I'm sticking with it! Give it a try.

POWER UP WITH PRAYER

Mary L. Maxson
Associate Pastor, Pastor for Nurture & Discipleship,
Paradise Seventh-day Adventist Church
Paradise, California

Within our church life, ministry is a gift from God. It can be expressed by an equation: [*ministry = service = Christianity*]. I would love for our members to desire with all their hearts to be involved in ministry, just as they desire to be connected with God. However, the reality is that unless members have caught a glimpse of the equation [*ministry = service = being a church member*] there will always be a struggle to match the ministry gift with the member.

It is my dream to see members so in love with Jesus that they automatically choose to serve. Below are some of the ministry areas in which I have been involved throughout my eight years as an associate pastor. In all the ministries in which I am involved, prayer is the primary resource along with the guidance of the Holy Spirit. Prayer is a flame, and the Holy Spirit is my power!

EMPOWERING MINISTRY TEAM (EMT). As a pastoral staff, we felt it was rather redundant to nominate a nominating committee to nominate people to serve in ministry. Instead, we have accomplished the process of matching ministry with member with our Empowering Ministry Team (EMT). This team is itself a ministry formed around five years ago. The emphasis of the EMT is to match the member's spiritual gift to the area of ministry which utilizes that God-given gift. EMT has had some growing pains, but it is beginning to function more smoothly as time goes along. A member gifted in administration was chosen as the chairperson, and I, as pastor, serve as a liaison for this ministry.

MINISTRY FAIRE. We have also conducted a yearly "Ministry Faire" which has been quite successful. The Faire features exhibits of all the church ministries that chose to participate. Each exhibit provides a tri-fold explaining its ministry—the spiritual gift involved in that ministry, and a description of its work. Then when members come by, the ministry leader can explore with them where they might best serve.

DISCIPLING WOMEN. God has gifted me with the gift of active listening and the ability to perceive where a woman is in her Christian journey. I have prepared "Discipling Points" which I use when I disciple women. There isn't space here to go into details, but I would be willing to provide guidelines (for all ages) to those who would like to have them. How do I know whom to disciple? I spend time in prayer, asking God to bring me in contact with persons for whom I can add God-value to their lives. As a result, I am discipling individuals of all ages—from 7 to 95.

On my first discipling visit, I use a spiritual assessment that has been extremely beneficial. This process zeros in on areas where the individual might need discipling. I depend totally on the Holy Spirit to guide me. The Holy Spirit gives me direction and the questions to ask. The Holy Spirit and the person to be discipled direct the agenda. As God directs individuals to me, I bathe them in prayer. God's name is glorified through the ministry as I partner with Him. My mission is to passionately love Jesus as He guides me to nurture and disciple individuals, providing them opportunities to see themselves through the eyes of Jesus.

SELF DISCIPLINE AND PRAYER

Sharon Jefferson
Bible Worker/ Evangelist

Self discipline means to exercise power over one's self—self mastery over one's inner desires, actions, words, and thoughts.

When we read and study the Bible, we are gaining insight into God's character. In return, we have a responsibility, not only to represent Him, but to "re-present" Him to others by putting His way into action in our lives. Ministry has many challenges—unfairness, jealousy, criticism, and discord. And it tempts us to want to handle problems in our own strength. But we need to learn to stay focused on what God has called us to do. God's reputation and character suffers each time we face adversity and do not handle it properly.

We pray and ask God to handle a situation, but, when we allow people and obstacles to highlight our shortcomings, we let Satan take the credit.

God wants the fruit of the Spirit to be magnified in our lives so powerfully that evil is overcome with good. He is able to be involved in any situation and accomplish His purpose and His will, but only if we are willing to relinquish our will wholeheartedly and trust Him to fight for us as Lord of our lives. When our prayers are unanswered, the problem is not with God; the problem lies with us. God works in all of life's situations to manifest His character. When He decides to step in, He will show Himself strong on our behalf.

Our aim should be to represent Christ's character to others. People are looking for an outlet to plug into, for power to deal with life's situations. As they see how we handle life, they decide whether or not they want to plug into the power that is flowing through us. We may be the only Bible some people read. So we have to be careful. We need to find a way to surrender self and let God be in control. Life is never primarily about the situation we are dealing with; it's about revealing God's ability to deal with every aspect of our lives.

Satan knows that if we rely on God's power, we already have the victory. He also knows that we are the only ones who can disrupt God's planned outcome for each situation. Therefore Satan plays on our weaknesses in order to discredit God's character. We need to bring all our character flaws into harmony with the Word of God. When the enemy throws us a stumbling block—a distraction—and we act contrary to God's Word, it gives Satan the upper hand. Therefore in order for us to get the victory, we have to take our hands off and let God put his hands on. Only God can make wrongs right.

Don't allow circumstances to define you. Let the Holy Spirit define you, so that you may know the difference between God's peace and the transitory peace the world offers. In every situation, ask yourself, "What would Jesus do?" God wants His character to shine through us! He wants us to stand steadfast and handle situations properly. Standing for principle and persevering to the end exposes the true condition of the heart. Passion and ministry can make you do "crazy" things—like continuing to pray and exercise faith when you want to give up or like denying self, because you know there is a bigger cause at stake.

That's why it's important to spend time alone with God. That's why it's important to have other clergy women standing alongside you to pour courage into you, to undergird you, to lift you up, and to counsel you. Self discipline is important because it indicates Christian maturity. Without it, we become unfit and fail in ministry.

Believe me, you will experience many teachable moments. If you fail, don't stop. Use each failure as a learning experience. Remember: "When you know better, you do better." Learn to respect the call God has made on your life. Walk in freedom. Don't walk on eggshells, waiting to see who is watching you; just practice what you preach!

To sum it all up: You're never the tallest until you fight every battle on your knees. It's not about you; it's about God. The battle is not yours; it is the Lord's.

Ministry simply humbles you! And that's how ministry works for me.

SENSITIVITY, FLEXIBILITY, AND JESUS

Karen Lewis
Bible Worker Trainer and Associate Pastor,
Stillwater Seventh-day Adventist Church
Minnesota Conference

Being a female pastor in the Seventh-day Adventist Church is not an easy undertaking. Years of tradition have made it more difficult for older congregations to be accepting of a female as a pastor. However with sensitivity, flexibility, and love it can be accomplished.

I am the associate pastor of a small church in Minnesota. The lead pastor attends this church only four times a year, so for all intents and purposes I am the pastor even though I am the "associate" and pastor only part time (I typically preach twice a month).

One of the things I have found to be most effective in my pastoral work is to be sensitive and caring to the needs of the congregation. Change is difficult for most people, and your presence as a female pastor may be confusing to them. They know how to relate to a male pastor, but it can be confusing—especially for the male elders in your congregations—to know how to relate to a female pastor. It takes time to develop a relationship with your leaders; you will need to earn their trust and respect. Treating them with respect and sensitivity will go a long way—as will a sense of humor.

So, in a nutshell, here are the key points I have found helpful in getting the congregation to accept and respect me:

1. **LISTEN TO MEMBERS FULLY.** Don't automatically tune them out if you don't agree with them. They need to be heard.

2. **EMPATHIZE WITH MEMBERS.** They need to feel understood. Know where they're coming from. Understand where they're coming from. This will go a long way to helping them feel that you care about them and their needs.

3. **BUILD BRIDGES.** Learn enough about your members to discover shared interests and other things you and they have in common. Visit them in their homes. Meet them for lunch. You can't disciple people unless you have first fostered a relationship with them.

4. **BE DEPENDABLE.** One of the fastest ways to erode trust is to fail to be reliable. Make sure to follow through on projects or promises. Let members know that they can depend on you.

5. **RETURN PHONE CALLS QUICKLY.** In today's society it is not unusual for folks to get back with us four to five days later. That sends a signal that our phone call is not important and neither are we. I always try to call members back the same day—and within the next hour if possible.

6. **LIFT UP JESUS IN EVERY SERMON.** He is where the power comes from, and members will really appreciate your sermons if Jesus, not you, is the main focus. People are starving for the bread of life. Jesus said, "And I, if I am lifted up from the earth will draw all men unto myself."—NASB. Let the Holy Spirit do the work that He needs to do in your members' lives, and you will be blessed.

Trust takes time, and one of the biggest ways to blow trust is to start making changes immediately. If you do this, in essence you are saying that everything that was accomplished in that church before you came was not important—and that is rather arrogant.

In conclusion, the members of your congregation really do want to like and respect you. Make it easy for them to do this. Give them the respect and love they deserve, and make sure you are lifting up Jesus to them each Sabbath. In time, you will have the church behind you, and you will be able to lead by making those needed changes that the Lord is placing on your heart.

SUCCESS THROUGH SURRENDER

Jennifer Woody
Youth Pastor
Pacific Union College Seventh-day Adventist Church

I remember standing in the middle of the academy campus where I had recently been called to serve and feeling that the task before me was insurmountable. I had recently graduated with my theology degree and had been called to be a dean at Auburn Adventist Academy in Auburn, Washington. We were one month into the school year when a turn of events placed the position of campus chaplain in my lap, along with all of my regular duties as a dean. So, here I was—standing in the middle of a campus that was not only reeling from a crisis, but spiritually depleted and discouraged. And, somehow, I was supposed to spiritually lead students and faculty.

"God," I said, "I'm not sure what You are doing or why You have called me here, and I know I am not up to this task. The students don't know me, and I have inherited a campus ministries team who doesn't trust me and who want their old chaplain back."

As I was standing there praying, crying, throwing up my hands in desperation, God reminded me of a card that a dear friend had given me when she had learned I had accepted the call to Auburn. The message on the front of the card said, "Attempt something so big that failure is imminent, unless God steps in." As the Holy Spirit brought this to my mind, I trembled. This was a task way too big for me; there was no way I was going to be able to do what needed to be done. I was just one person—and a new person on campus at that.

As I was complaining about all of this to the Lord, He gently reminded me that yes, He was well aware of the situation and that He knew I could not succeed—but He would. And succeed He did. He stepped in and turned the situation around for His glory, reminding me to surrender and let Him be God.

When I look back on my ministry, the times of greatest success were the impossible situations when I had to let go and let God take control. How often we, as women, feel like we need to be in control—or at least look and act like we are in control. So many times in an effort to prove ourselves as valuable instruments to His work, we ask God to step aside while we show the world that we can do what He has called us to do.

Yet success in our ministries comes when we surrender to who He is and to His Word. I do not know what you are personally facing in your ministry, but God does, and His Word has the answers. Joshua 1:7, 8 says, "Only be strong and very courageous; be careful to do according to all the law which Moses My servant commanded you; do not turn from it to the right hand or to the left, so that you may have success wherever you go. This book of the law shall not depart from your mouth, but you shall meditate on it day and night, so that you may be careful to do according to all that is written in it; for then you will make your way prosperous, and then you will have success."NASB. Also Job 22:21

says, "Yield [surrender] now and be at peace with Him; thereby good will come to you."—NASB. In yielding up ourselves good will come; we will produce good fruit. It's interesting that just as the words, yield and surrender, are synonymous in one sense, they are related in yet a broader way. Yield can mean "to surrender," but it can also mean "to produce." And spiritually we cannot truly produce fruit without surrendering.

As we practice being completely God-dependent, yielding our will to His will, He will multiply our efforts in ways we could have never imagined. John the Baptist found the secret to success. He said of Jesus, "He must increase, but I must decrease."—John 3:30.—NASB.

May you and your ministry be blessed as, in His strength, you do just that.

THE CALENDAR

Paula Oliver, DMin
Pastor
First Seventh-day Adventist Church of Montclair

Being assigned to your first district can be a nerve racking experience. Before your installation, you may spend a lot of nights concerned about how you will perform. How will your leadership be received? How will you handle board meetings if someone decides to challenge you? There is a long list of potential concerns and disasters that may run through your mind. Instead of getting lost in the land of what ifs, realize that pastoring is less about your performance and more about building up the church. Getting caught up in power struggles, infighting, and playing referee between ministries can seriously hamper the ministry of the church as a whole. As a pastor, your responsibility is to not lose sight of the big picture.

Remember the church has a corporate identity. I discovered early in my ministry that my role as a pastor was akin to being the mayor of a small town. Municipalities are comprised of various departments such as Health, Social Services, Community Services, Building, Finances, Municipal Clerk, etc. As matter of fact, these offices look similar to the ministries that make up a typical church board. Just as a mayor must equip and manage each municipal department, so the church pastor has to manage, equip, and empower each local ministry.

The pastor must figure out a way to coalesce the talents of her leaders, have ministries work in harmony with one another, and provide direction for the church. One way to accomplish these goals is to have a carefully thought through church calendar.

I picked up this idea while being an associate pastor and after conversing with other successful pastors. It is helpful to have a calendar with monthly themes and "boilerplate" events. By the latter, I mean the church calendar should have standardized ministry events that the church members learn to anticipate and prepare for. For example, at the church I currently pastor, we consider January as a time of renewal. So we begin each year with a twenty-one-day "Daniel Fast." Early in the year is also a perfect time to have an annual lunch honoring the new members who have joined the church during the previous year.

February can be a month to celebrate Black History, with each Sabbath being assigned to a particular group of the Black Diaspora. Alternatively, the month of February can be a month that celebrates love or relationships in general. March is often a standard time for Youth Week of Prayer. April can be a time to present a doctrinal series. Around Easter time, the church can hold a "Seven Last Words" series with guest preachers. September is evangelism month, October celebrates church history; in November the church honors God with Thanksgiving, etc. As ministry leaders submit their events for the year, each event can be scheduled for a month that shares a theme with that event.

The calendar must also remain flexible. Guest speakers may cancel at the last minute; some ministry teams may need more time to prepare for their event. Things happen. It is okay to reshuffle some events. Consequently, the pastor should give calendar updates at every monthly board meeting. Overall, however, it is best to try to limit changes so that the calendar will have a sense of regularity.

If you are worried that a predictable calendar may become boring to the saints, I and my colleagues have not found that to be the case. To the contrary, we have found that predictability builds stability. People like knowing what is going to happen next. Keep in mind that the timing of the events may be predictable, but the event itself can be carried out in many creative ways.

In summary, ministry events should not be sporadic "flash in the pan" ideas so that after one event is completed, people sit around waiting for another bright idea to be suddenly revealed. Having a themed calendar incorporates each idea as part of a greater collective initiative in serving and saving souls.

Being a spiritual mayor is very demanding. However, one of my ministry mentors taught me that in the local church, if you are not leading, someone else is. You will find that having a solid plan—reflected in a strategic calendar and setting a direction for the church—helps to engender confidence in your leadership.

THE POWER OF RELATIONSHIPS

Lisa Engelkemier
Executive Pastor, Newday Seventh-day Adventist Church
Parker, Colorado

God created us for intimate connection in relationships. In those times when we're fortunate enough to experience relationships in which we connect intimately, those interactions deeply affect us for good. That goodness touches us mentally, emotionally, socially, and even physically. Needless to say, relationship is a powerful tool in God's hands.

Upon arriving at a young church seven years ago, one of my first assignments was to visit each member, preferably in their home. Since I naturally tend to be relational and warm, I looked forward to the assignment. The most challenging part, however, turned out to be finding my way around and through large subdivisions. Sometimes, these visits took place over a dinner. Sometimes, we simply talked in the comfort of a living room. But always, visits were unhurried. I was there to become acquainted. Stories and experiences were shared in safety and without judgment. We talked about things that mattered and discovered we had things in common. We opened up about experiences that we found meaningful or painful or frustrating. These visits were the important beginnings of relationships in which there was mutual trust and understanding, and they created a strong foundation for ministry.

Relationships continued to be developed as ministry teams were established and systems were created. Relationships deepened through sharing meals, conversation, and life. Relationship opened the way to dream together about ministry possibilities and what it might look like to pursue those dreams together. Other relationships grew into spiritual friendships, life changes, and eventually baptisms. Relationship has made difficult conversations easier to hear.

I've discovered that relationships need to be protected, prioritized, and cared for, because we live in a culture that prizes independence and rugged individualism. The New Testament teachings on what relationship is to look like among Christians have become foreign and unnatural to us today. Relationship needs to be learned, and the church needs to be the place in which we learn, together. The church needs a variety of safe environments where, together, in genuine Christian relationship, we can share genuinely, pray boldly, forgive freely, give generously, and serve wholeheartedly.

My ministry style continues to be highly relational. I find meaning in unhurried interaction in which people have been heard and understood—an encounter that leaves them knowing they matter. But, how does one sustain a relationship-based ministry when life is full of the unexpected and holds more than we can surround? I've discovered that it happens when I'm intentional about prioritizing practices that support personal wellbeing. I've discovered that a collection of practices such as journaling, reading and reflecting on Scripture, walking, bike riding, and meaningful time with friends keeps me renewed and increases my capacity to be present in relationship.

Two other practices that, for me, have enhanced relationships in ministry are becoming educated on personality styles so that I relate in ways that honor others and deepening skills in crucial conversations in order to be full of grace toward the individual, while speaking truth. In my opinion and experience, relationships are powerful. Developing relationships and caring for them are absolutely a ministry best practice.

THOUGH SHE IS BUT SMALL…

Jenniffer Ogden
Youth Pastor
Pacific Union College Seventh-day Adventist Church

Leaves crunched under foot, and huffs of breath tinted the air around our heads a wispy gray-blue. The soft fiber of the couch slipped and slid in our hands. A grunt leapt out of my mouth as I hefted my end higher and walked up the ramp of the truck. Sitting on the curb later, munching on hunks of pizza, we joked and compared new scrapes and cuts on hands and shins. As I lurched, crablike, off the curb, pawed my keys out of my pocket, and began to head to my car after rounds of hugs, a firm handshake held me in place. "I have never met a pastor who would help anyone move before. You're cool."

I walked away that day exhausted, sore, and in need of antibiotic ointment. But the words from that young woman have followed me for years.

Moments of crisis (big surgeries, funerals) and times of great celebration (baptisms, weddings) are the *common* times for the pastor to be present. These are wonderful times to be supportive and helpful. Days in the office are important to healthy Bible studies, depth in sermons, and efficient, God-focused communication.

But moments of insignificance are the *essential* times for a pastor to be present. The hours spent bouncing on the trampoline, hauling boxes, cheering at a high school dance recital, baking cookies and delivering them—these are small moments in life, but when one shows up for the small moments, one is much more able to be truly helpful in the big moments. The moments that seem insignificant are, in fact, the biggest part of the journey.

The child that cuddles next to me at Children's Story on Sabbath morning is the one who joyfully showed me her pumpkin painting at school that week. The woman who grabs me after church for a time of prayer in my office is the one I missed at church last week—and my call to her is what let her know that her presence makes a difference.

After years of wearing the title of pastor, I have learned to show up for the insignificant times, so that when the big moments come, I am not the awkward stranger. I'm family.

And right now, the stack of boxes and stash of ointment growing in my closet at home is ready for the next move.

USING EVENTS TO BUILD BRIDGES

Chanda M. Nunes
Associate Pastor for Evangelism, Outreach, Member Care, and Young Adult Ministry
New Haven Seventh-day Adventist Church
Overland Park, Kansas

For a pastor or ministry leader, there is nothing more discouraging and frustrating than planning outreach opportunities for your congregation and not having the participation you had hoped for or the impact you planned to have on the community. If that has ever happened to you, as it has to me, you question, "Why even continue?"

I have been blessed to be one of the pastors at New Haven Church, in Overland Park, Kansas, that has hosted several successful outreach events. Each year, for the past fourteen years, we have hosted more than a thousand community guests in our church in a single, non-traditional outreach event. And our members have participated in great numbers. The event is called *Safe Haven*, and it takes place on Halloween Night

(I know that just shocked someone). Using Bible-themed interactive rooms, fun activities for the family, and sharing treats (including religious literature for all ages), we provide a safe venue and minister to our community at a time when people are very open to participate.

What are some of the lessons we have learned with this event? Are there principles that can be transferred to any context? How does a ministry leader provide programming that involves the church and affects the community? Here are some of the answers to those questions.

RECRUIT VOLUNTEERS. Start with who you have and what you have. Realize that not everyone will be on board initially, and not everyone will ever be on board—and that's okay. Be sure to ask members what they feel comfortable doing to participate in the programming. Maybe they can pray, donate items, assist with decorating, stuff bags, greet guests, or assist with set-up and take-down. The bottom line: give everyone an opportunity to play a role in the programming you provide. Allow the community to take ownership as well. I know you may see this as "risky." But if you meet the felt needs of the community for long enough, eventually the community will partner with you through its time, influence, and yes, its money!

Safe Haven has been designed to have numerous opportunities for participation so that many members can serve where their gifts fit best. This past year, we had neighboring Christian churches that donated money and even sent volunteers to assist us.

USE ADVERTISING THAT WORKS FOR YOUR COMMUNITY. Every community has a type of advertising that works best. The reality is that mailings cost big dollars and often produce little returns. You can use community-access television channels, and your local newspaper may place free notices of community events. Social media is another great and affordable method of advertising, as well as banners, email blasts, and personal invitations. However, the "real deal" key is consistency. Your best advertising is your track record. If you have a successful event, repeat it yearly! Yes, this will take commitment, planning, continued donations, and people-power, but if you put on the event annually, I guarantee that eventually it will get to the point where advertising is no longer necessary, because your event is now known and recognized as a major component of your community. We no longer have to advertise Safe Haven. In fact we would probably have to advertise if we were *not* having it.

PLAN THE EVENT FOR A HOLIDAY OR TO OCCUR AT THE SAME TIME EACH YEAR. As we know, people are more prone to attend church events/programming on special holidays—Easter, Christmas, New Year, etc.,. They are also more willing to open their doors on days when they would naturally open them. For example, host a canned goods collection on Halloween night for your church food pantry or local food bank. Utilize these opportunities as much as possible to host events and programming at your church that will benefit the community and ultimately draw people to attend weekly services.

Ride the wave that these events generate in the community. People who may not be open to church look for things to do during the holidays. Take advantage of this to reach your community and build relationships.

ASK BIG. As agents of God, if we are going to further His cause, we can't be afraid to ask big! My general rule of thumb is: *"Ask first, then utilize the budget only if necessary."* When you have determined what you need, first ask members to search their homes, offices, storage units, etc. for the items you need. Second, utilize local thrift stores before touching the budget! Solicit local stores for donations and be sure to bring a donation letter with you. Also, ask your conference if funding is available.

With new programming, you may have to use donations from your members and even the church budget *(last resort)*, but after you have built up a track record, local businesses and individuals will be open to give to an event they see has benefited the community. I have seen some unbelievable donations over the past few years. *Safe Haven* has now gotten to the place where it does not use church operating funds at all.

We have great news to share with our communities. We have awesome ministries that we want to have an impact on them. We need to build bridges so that we can share this good news and good works. Using outreach events can create those bridges. Let's continue to get out there.

VIVA LA DIFFERENCE!

Courtney Ray, Pastor
Breath of Life Seventh-day Adventist Church

When I was an undergrad, I took a homiletics class wherein the professor advised the female students to pull their hair back while preaching so it wouldn't be "distracting." Over the years I've heard many well-meaning bits of advice from both men and women who believed that the best way to encourage women in ministry was to help them "blend in." I've heard gems such as making sure my voice isn't too high, ensuring that my shoe heels are low enough, and of course, confining my wardrobe to dark "masculine" colors like blue, black, and brown. The success to being a pastor apparently depends on making sure people aren't reminded of your femaleness.

Now there's nothing wrong with wearing your hair back (I often do, anyway) or having a voice in a lower register (if it's naturally that way) or wearing low heels (after all, you are standing up for a long time). But if the idea is to obscure who you are in order to make sure people don't notice that you are "different," then that's a problem.

Many pastors—both men and women—fall into the trap of trying to emulate other pastors in order to replicate success. But I definitely subscribe to Oscar Wilde's advice that you ought to "be yourself since everyone else is already taken!"

Over time, I have begun to shed the restrictive ideas of superficial "sameness." And my professional development has involved much more than simply adopting a more colorful wardrobe! As I have grown into my own pastoral rhythms, I've learned that although many preachers are awesome at "runs" and some pastors live by manuscripts, those things don't work for me. I found that God has given me a gift for illustration, and I often employ visual aids and props to bring a message to life. God has used those sermons to be not only enjoyable, but memorable for the congregations I've preached to. People have often talked about how they remembered something that helped them in their time of need from "the sermon with the engine" or "the sermon with the soda cans." And wonder of all wonders, they remembered my sermons in spite of my occasional bright-colored suits!

My preaching style has evolved as a function of how God has best gifted me. I am able to reach people who are visual and tactile learners and engage them in ways that many other preachers do not. If I had merely focused on replicating the methods of others, I would have neglected the unique ways that God wants to use me as an individual.

I invite pastors, especially those who are beginning their ministry, to not worry about fitting into some pre-prescribed mold. Yes, that may mean that people will notice that you're "different." But that may be exactly what God intends to use!

YOUR STORY. THEIR STORY. OUR STORY.

Massiel Davila-Ferrer
Pastor of Nurture, College Heights Seventh-day Adventist Church
Lacombe, Alberta, Canada

Know yourself . . .

It was my first camp pitch, and I eagerly put on my brand new work gloves and went to join my team in unloading the benches and setting them up in the main auditorium. As my turn came to carry one side of the benches, I realized they were heavy and my colleagues were strong. After two more failed attempts I had to let go of my pride and the idea that I was going to be able to help in this task. I stood there taking in the scene and wondering if these guys thought I was going to use my gender as an excuse to be a slacker.

While standing there, arguing with no one, I noticed the benches were dirty. I knew no woman in her Sabbath best would want to sit down on a dirty seat, so I asked if cleaning them was part of our job, too. When I got a shrug in response, I took that as my cue to get to work. While I washed and wiped and dusted, I had some help moving benches around so that they were gleaming in gloriously symmetrical rows. I learned that I can't always do the same thing "they" can, and "they" may not always see the same things I do. But together, working from our strengths, we can do a better more complete work.

Know your story . . .

"You have three strikes against you. You're young. You're ethnic. You're female." I'd heard this assessment more than once, but it has been my experience that these three "strikes" are my strengths—perhaps my greatest ones. These qualifications propel me to platforms where my voice is amplified and I get to represent our church more widely. When I was studying for ministry, I didn't look like my classmates, or sound like them, or preach like them. I had no one to copy. I had to let God create a new type of pastor in me. When we let go of the perceived expectations of what a pastor looks and sounds like, we begin to let God have the opportunity to do a brand new thing in us.

The door right now is wide open for you . . .

Lead from your feminine identity. Lead from your culture and background. Lead from a place of nurture or organization, of creativity or logic, or all of the above—if you are so gifted. Whatever you're strength is, lead from there. Lead from your uniqueness. Do not try to change your personality to match your position. You, in your skin, with all of your unique characteristics, were called to ministry. You in your heels or flats, pants suit, skirt suit, or dress were called. Do not change to fit your ministry. God will refine your character, your personality—and your sense of style is part of the package.

Know where your stories overlap . . .

As I walked by two pastors in deep conversation, I overheard one say in a defeated tone, "I'm just feeling frustrated, because they're not taking me seriously. They are doubting my call to ministry." For a moment the thought, "How does that feel?" fueled my skewed sense of justice. In time, however, hearing the words I'd heard so many of my female colleagues utter coming from a young man made me understand that we are all going to have pieces of the same story. We are all going to have people doubt us, challenge us, and belittle us. Because ministry is hard. It's hard for women. It's hard for men. Ministry is hard. When we listen to our brothers with the same empathy we want for ourselves, we can change how pieces of the story unfold. We can write a new narrative of how men and women do ministry together.

CALLED

Tara J. VinCross, DMin.
Director, REACH Columbia Union Urban Evangelism School and
Senior Pastor of REACH Philadelphia Seventh-day Adventist Church

5 years ago I set out on a journey to write and implement a discipleship group curriculum in the local church where I served as senior pastor. I wanted to intentionally provide a space for people to grow in their relationship with God and the way they engaged in His mission.

As we know, discipleship is not another program of the church - something members can check off on their spiritual "to do" list. Instead it is the essential process of transformation into Christlikeness that takes place in relationship with God and other believers. The goal is to form disciples, who make disciples, who make disciples - spreading the passion, love, and service of Christ.

As Adventists, we are called to proclaim a message of scriptural truth. Yet, scripture itself paints a compelling picture of a healthy church living and breathing primarily through a love relationship with Jesus. It is this personal encounter, and not merely information about God, which in turn draws others to want to experience Jesus for themselves. Christ's appeal to the church is to move beyond a lukewarm religion and into an authentic relationship (Rev 3:14-20), which leads others to come and experience Him themselves (Jn 4:42).

Over time, I was able to develop a curriculum and invite a group of adventurous souls to join me for the journey. The group formed and went through the curriculum for 12-weeks. Class sessions used a combination of one-on-one accountability, small group process, experiential teaching time, discussion, and personal devotional exercises (prayer, praise, devotional reading of scripture, etc.). At the end of the process, every church member who participated stated that they had experienced a deeper devotional life and ministry involvement as a result of their participation! They described a new willingness to step out of their comfort zone to engage with other people. They spoke of a prayer life that was not only focused on what they wanted from God but also praised God for who He is. They realized an openness to trust other people beyond what they had been willing to do before. It was really incredible to witness what God did!

On this journey, I discovered my own desire for a short cut. As a pastor I was still searching for a 'magic bullet' that would rapidly change members into Christlikeness and grow the church numerically. I wanted transformation in a rush. Turns out, God's invitation was for me to abide and let God do the work. There is no shortcut to growth. Change takes time. Transformation takes making time in community for people to encounter the Living God This is something only the Holy Spirit can work in the life. I, as pastor, can facilitate transformation by creating opportunities where people can experience God. There is, however, no shortcut for the slow change that comes by consistently being in God's presence. I have discovered peace in God's promise to finish the work that has been started in each person (Phil 1:6).

The good news is, when we as pastors are intentional about discipling believers in what it looks like to be in relationship with God, it makes a difference! The devotional life and level of involvement in the mission of the church increases among the members who are participating. This discipleship approach, though slow, is lasting.

If you're wondering how you could implement a discipleship process, first think specifically about how you pray, how you connect with God in the Word, how you fast, how you praise, and then talk to people about those specific hows. Next provide space for people to practice in God's presence. Finally, complete the learning cycle by having them share their learning and growth with one another.

God brought about dramatic change in my own life and ministry through this process. I would not say that I have it all figured out. In fact, I am now asking new questions while exploring what it means to focus on discipleship in the local church, and especially what my role is as pastor in this process. Still, even with more to learn, I can see that in heart and mind I have grown, even as the participants experienced growth in their own relationships with God. There is nothing like watching the transforming work of the Holy Spirit in someone's life!

WOMEN IN PASTORAL MINSTRY

Michelle Hill
Pastor, Pembroke Seventh-day Adventist Church
Bermuda Conference of Seventh-day Adventists

Pastoral ministry can be the source of great joy and fulfillment, and it can also be the source of great sorrow and anxiety. Why? Because it involves people. All kinds of people with different personalities, different ideas and different worldviews. I have found two simple practices to be highly effective. Firstly, get to know your members, get to know them intimately. Spend time learning who they are, their families, and the experiences that have shaped their lives. There is a very real temptation to be so consumed with administration, program planning and sermonic preparation that we neglect what matters most, the sheep. I remind myself daily that my role is to shepherd the flock, a good shepherd knows their sheep, he or she knows where they are spiritually; the shepherd knows their present state of affairs. Sheep are easier to minister to when you understand them, they respond more readily to you when they know that you genuinely care. The complexities of ministry, which includes conflict resolution is far less complicated when genuine relationships have been established. People listen when they know you care.

Once you get to know your members, love them. There is a song that says "What the world needs now is love sweet love." What the church needs now is love sweet love- from their pastor! Love has a greater impact than any sermon or program ever could. Love them inspite of their flaws, their behaviors, the reality is that sheep are not always nice, sometimes they can be downright mean and stubborn! They can draw blood and tears. I have found that these are the ones that need extra hugs, more phone calls, more time and tender words. We can be tempted to take personally the unpleasant behaviors projected onto us by our members, but remember your role is to stand with them, to encourage them and to lead them in the path of righteous. If the shepherd disengages who will lead the sheep? The enemy will often use behaviors to discourage us, to cause us to withdraw from difficult sheep, this is when you need to pray for extra grace for yourself and them. Your loving will not be in vain, it will spill over onto your members who will in turn love you back. Remember, the river can rise no higher than its source, the attitude you display will be mirrored by your members. The Lord is our shepherd, He will lead you the undershepherd in the path of still waters and lead you in the path of righteousness. Feed His sheep with love.